Books by Samuel K. Anderson

1. God's Audacity: The Logic of God's Existence.

2. Whispers from My Mother.

3. Human's Audacity: The Leadership in Everyone.

4. The Kind Prince and Princess (Children's Book edition)

5. Ascend to your higher self

ASCEND TO YOUR HIGHER SELF

By

Samuel K. Anderson

Royal Publication
New Jersey, U.S.A

Copyright © 2020 Samuel K. Anderson.

All rights reserved. No part of this book may be reproduced or used in any manner without written permission of the copyright owner except for the use of quotations in a book review.

2nd Edition 2020

ISBN-13: 978-1-7340066-1-2 Paperback Edition

Royal Publication

royalpublication@aol.com

Website: royalpublication.net

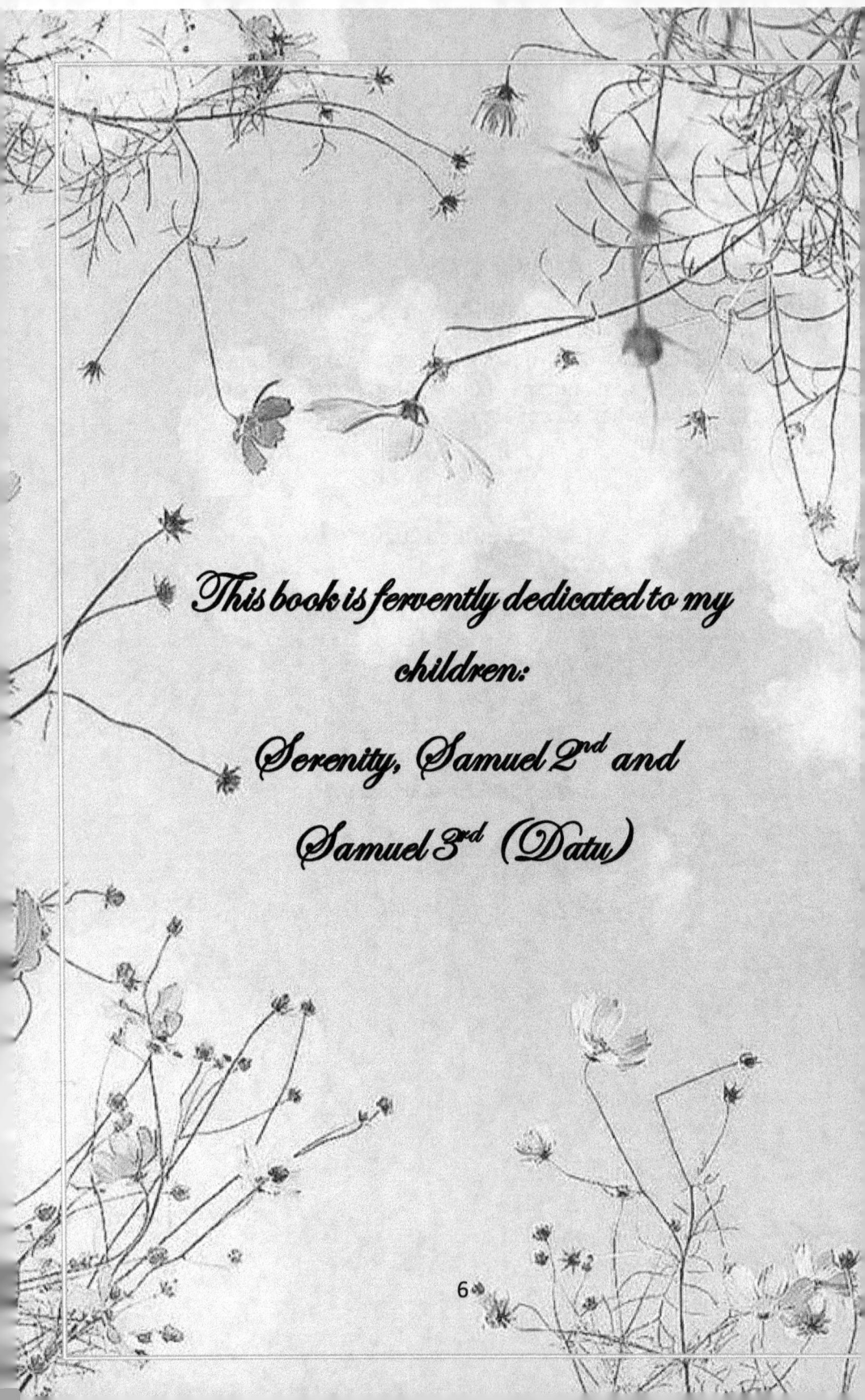

This book is fervently dedicated to my children:

Serenity, Samuel 2nd and

Samuel 3rd (Datu)

Introduction

Ascend to your higher self unfolds the power of your ascension.

This book teaches you how to use your inner self to catapult to your desired level of ascension.

Failing to have control over your higher self may put you disproportionately out of your frequency.

Your ascension is your power. Hence, use your ascension wisely in order to attract the right energy.

Feel your Ascension.
Adore your Ascension.
Embrace your Ascension.
Love your Ascension.
Use your ascension for your redemption.

Table of Content

Chapter 1: Vision

Chapter 2: Soul

Chapter 3: Trust

Chapter 4: EVF

Chapter 5: Civil

Chapter 6: Fear

Chapter 7: Lion

Chapter 8: Past

Chapter 9: Love

Chapter 10: Live

Chapter 11: Money

Chapter 12: True

Chapter 13: Own

Chapter 14: Eye

Chapter 15: Money

Chapter 16: Exit

Chapter 17: Go

Chapter 18: Nature

Chapter 19: Energy

Chapter 20: Sand

Chapter 21: Only

Chapter 22: Time

Chapter 23: Begin

Chapter 24: Weapon

Chapter 25: Know

Chapter 26: Master

Chapter 27: Mind

Chapter 28: Keys

Chapter 29: God

Chapter 30: Panic

Ascend to Your Higher Self.

Chapter 1

A vision with a mission on a mission misses not its vision.

— Samuel K. Anderson

Ascend to Your Higher Self.

Be focus and fully certain about your journey. There is a popular old saying ascribed to Lao Tzu that goes like this: *a journey of a thousand miles only begins with a step.*

When you have your vision married with a mission that is set on a strong indisputable mission in action then your vision will not be missed because you have your mind made up.

Ascend to Your Higher Self.

Chapter 2

The Spirit of the Soul is in its Spirituality.

Samuel K. Anderson

Ascend to Your Higher Self.

You are a dead soul without spirituality. Spirituality is a way of life of your spirit (that is your true self). The soul needs to connect with either its spirit or its flesh.

You have the power to decide to give in to your flesh or into your spirit. When the soul is in alignment with your spirit, you tend to be more aware of your purpose. In this situation, you know who you are, why you are here, how to live life and you tend to be clear about the afterlife. Fear is completely seen as an illusion. You live life with passion, certainty and joy.

Ascend to Your Higher Self.

Chapter 3

Confidence breeds Resilience which in turn produces Excellence.

— Samuel K. Anderson

Ascend to Your Higher Self.

Self-assurance within your qualities or abilities to execute a specified activity or duty is very important in life. This is a trait that needs to be mastered if you dare to succeed in life.

Regardless of how tough or easy it gets, make sure to remain steadfast in confidence. Do not confuse confidence with arrogance. Be humble in your pursuit, use grit when needed to dig deep. Overtime, your confidence would build resilience and your resilience will eventually produce excellence. Desire for excellence not perfection.

Ascend to Your Higher Self.

Chapter 4

Spirituality is the absolute Frequency that Vibrates your Energy.

— Samuel K. Anderson

Ascend to Your Higher Self.

Think about it very well. Make sure to feel the essence of it in your core.

Now, I want to break it to you that you are a living spirit moving in your own frequency that propels you to vibrate within the infinity realms of energies. The quality of your survival is connected to your spirituality.

The earth and entire universe (which you are a part of) move through the absolute frequency of spirituality. To be truly liberated is to be spiritually and psychologically emancipated.

Ascend to Your Higher Self.

Pay attention to your energy when it vibrates at different frequency levels in order to detect your spirituality. You cannot muscle through spirituality. It is natural.

You have to be able to sense the energy, the vibration, the frequency. This realm is weightless, even a feather is heavy in this realm. Meaning you have to be lighter than a feather.

Vibrate your energy to an absolute frequency of your spirituality to be one with everything.

Ascend to Your Higher Self.

Chapter 5

To be civilized is to be forced either physically or psychologically to reject your culture and traditions.

—Samuel K. Anderson

Etymology of the word "civilized" is an early 17th century French origin. It became popular in the 1800s throughout the 1900s and declined steadily in usage and enforcement in the 2000s and beyond.

Synonymous to the word "civilized" is "acculturate" meaning the dominant culture will impose its ways on you to break you until you assimilate socially and psychologically.

Ascend to Your Higher Self.

You may eventually forget your own self, culture, and traditions including language, medicine, achievements, beliefs, et al.

Anyone who do not know himself/herself can easily be manipulated to believe literally anything.

Ascend to Your Higher Self.

Chapter 6

"Formal education" doesn't enhance your gift(s), rather it exposes your limitations and enhances the specialization of your fears.

~ Samuel K. Anderson

Education is not a *gift* and one's *gift* is not found in *education*. When a child is born, he/she has a *gift*, in some cases *gifts*. The child naturally develops his/her gift(s) under a conducive atmosphere without fear or favor.

If the child is allowed to develop his/her gifts without the influence of "systemic programed" fears of "school-job-retire-death" then his/her gifts will develop into his/her purpose on earth. Most people retire and at their dying bed, regardless of their achievements; they regret not living the life they had desired to live due to fear.

Rhetorically, why is that? Simply because most of us were never able to truly use our gifts to accomplish the reason(s) why we were born. Hence, we exit this planet regrettably unaccomplished.

Formal education is simply a "controlled" agenda of knowledge systemically

Ascend to Your Higher Self.

designed to manipulate the masses into believing that their own interest is protected without knowing that they are trading their priceless gifts just for pennies, nickels and dimes.

Informal education through the parents is an exception. Take this from me, your gifts see no fears, boundaries or limitations.

Ascend to Your Higher Self.

Chapter 7

A lion with a crown on its head without any subject is not a king of anyone but himself.

~Samuel K. Anderson

Ascend to Your Higher Self.

You can be materially wealthy but may lack the humility to lead, teach, influence and bless your own kind. A king is someone with the ability to lead in serve to others.

The people you help through service are the ones that confer kingship on you. Hence, the reason why they follow you and work with you for a common goal.

One can argue that, there is nothing wrong with just being a king of your own self. Although that may be true, it doesn't fulfil the essence, relevance or meaning of a true king. Being

Ascend to Your Higher Self.

the head of the household whereby your partner/wife and children follow your teachings, directions, and influence fulfills the essence of a king.

So, I say a lion without a crown but has subjects who believe in collective goal with a mission is a true king. Expressions of kingship are not necessarily in material exhibitions rather the services rendered to uplift, inspire, motivate and lead people to a higher frequency vibrating towards oneness with nature and the universe.

Ascend to Your Higher Self.

Chapter 8

The future is found in the past and the past rests in the future.

– Samuel K. Anderson

Ascend to Your Higher Self.

Everything is cyclical. Everything has a beginning, middle and an end before it re-sets. You can call it re-incarnation or regeneration if you ascribe to such frequency because that's exactly what it is.

Someone's beginning is another person's end and vice versa. Before there was formal business or education (pre and post flood), it used to be the community exchanging what they had for something they needed the most.

Massive trade formalities, technology, education, et al were birthed before the flood. We all started to rebuild, communicate, trade, educate, re-learn previous lives and technologies to aid us understand the "future" only to end up to where it all began all over again.

The infinity symbol ∞ summarizes the main point on this topic. We are all in a never-ending cyclical wave

Ascend to Your Higher Self.

of energy that vibrates as if it is spiral, yet the frequency pulls itself together to its infinite cyclical motion. The energy driving the universe shifts to a different form without changing its characteristics at the beginning of every cycle.

The future is just a shadow of the past. Solutions for the future is engraved in the past. There is no future without a past and no past without a future. What existed in the past is revealed

Ascend to Your Higher Self.

in the future which triggers a new beginning to reinstate the right frequencies. Currently, the earth and the universe are out of balance, damaged, and moving in opposite frequency. The energy needed to put things together is in hibernation. Everything will continue to be in chaos until the right shift of energy occurs to put things back into the right frequency.

Hence, the beginning from the end is initiated as a

Ascend to Your Higher Self.

resolution to all the chaos in the universe. We are all in what I call the infinite full cycle of energetic frequency vibrating through unseen wavelengths that repairs itself naturally.

Chapter 9

Terror begat terror. Love begat love. Love and Unity are the antithesis of greed, jealousy malice, chaos, and destruction.

~Samuel K. Anderson

Ascend to Your Higher Self.

Look around you, look deeper into your communities, districts, states, countries and our world. What do you see? We are stuck in a never-ending deception and delusion that everything is okay while our loved ones are murdered, robbed, disenfranchised, and with injustice hanging on our heads. We seek peace, love and unity in a terrorized state of affairs.

We walk around strapped with our guns, wanting peace and safety in our neighborhoods. Consciously, that's delusional and a psychological tranquilization of posttraumatic stress disorder (no insensitivity intended). I will leave the window open for your own assessment on this antithesis.

The darkness of today, the sunshine of tomorrow. Confusion and chaos precede calmness and solutions. At the heart of demoralization lies the vision of morality and the thirst to resolve all condescensions.

Ascend to Your Higher Self.

Chapter 10

We live in water within water in rhythmic frequency.

—Samuel K. Anderson

Ascend to Your Higher Self.

Water is everywhere around us. We use water every day. In actual fact, every living organism uses and lives in water. Moisture (moist) is water. Everything we do includes water in one state or another. The ocean is a massive collection of water bodies.

Our atmosphere is water in a different state. The air we breathe is filled with moisture that feeds our lungs aiding us to inhale and exhale. The foods we eat are mixed with water/saliva before it goes down into our stomachs. The human body is about seventy percent water.

Ascend to Your Higher Self.

Life is unbearable without a fertile land for agricultural purposes. Fertile lands need to be moist (needs water). Dry lands cannot support life. When living organisms lose water, they eventually die. Water supplies and sustains the nutrients in the soil. The moisture and nutrients help plants and other living organisms to grow. In turn, humans are fed. We are basically living in water within water in rhythmic frequency.

Chapter 11

Money is an illusion of power.

— Samuel K. Anderson

Money is not power, and power can never be money. However, money can be used in an illusive means to lure those with little to no morals to do the unthinkable. Money is not evil rather misunderstanding of money makes it evil. Hence, the root of all evil.

Money is energy. That's all it is. This simple statement is heavy to the world's populace. In that, majority of us do not understand that the kind of "energy" we give to money determines its behavior. We are all energy and everything around us is energy.

To have power doesn't mean you have money and to have money doesn't necessarily mean you have power. Power is a different kind of energy. Humans render their power to those with money, giving them the illusion of power. The illusion of power can be very destructive. Because power is given by the people to a leader or someone trustworthy. Our problem is our misunderstanding of money.

Chapter 12

True emancipation is the reversal of all the curses imposed on you spiritually, psychologically and physically.

– Samuel K. Anderson

Ascend to Your Higher Self.

You can never completely break anyone unless you are able to first and foremost break them spiritually, then psychologically and finally physically. The physical state of confusion is just the last and final result of the process of enslavement. The most powerful state of any human is his/her spiritual state. One's spiritual state is directly proportional in relatability to his/her psychological state. The physical wellbeing (appearance) is just an

Ascend to Your Higher Self.

illumination of your spiritual and psychological fortitude.

Study the tactics of colonization, the people did not just surrender. Absolutely not, they all fought hard and many nations won their freedom. All the colonizers established some form of religious monuments and teachings. This strategy was to cripple the colonized people spiritually. After that, their psychological fortitude was also crippled followed by

Ascend to Your Higher Self.

their physical enslavement. True emancipation starts with one's spiritual awakening, psychological and then finally physical.

Ascend to Your Higher Self.

Chapter 13

You are your own ancestor

– Samuel K. Anderson

Ascend to Your Higher Self.

When you physically die that means you have exited one door only to return through a different door. You then relearn everything. Time is an illusion; time is eternal, and you are in a recycling mode with the characteristic ability to multiply. Multiplication of you with the opposite sex exhibit a spiral unending repetition of reincarnation. This process hidden within our being can only be interrupted by the *Grand Master*, the *Creator*, the *Most High*, the *highest power of all energy* or the *Universe*.

Ascend to Your Higher Self.

If you are not punished or rewarded in this life then you may face your karma, reward or punishment in the repetitive cycle of life that you go through. You will never get away with any of the bad things you do. You will definitely be rewarded in one way or another with your good deeds. There is absolutely no escape until the finest level of pure purification is attained within the universe. You have been here before; you are your own ancestor.

Ascend to Your Higher Self.

Chapter 14

**Eye Sees
Eye Wants
Eye Desires
Eye Gets**

**Soul Sees
Soul Wants
Soul Desires
Soul Gets**

**Spirit Sees
Spirit Wants
Spirit Desires
Spirit Gets**

~Samuel K. Anderson

Ascend to Your Higher Self.

The eye, the soul, and the spirit are all in constant battle. They all see, want, desire, and get it at any means necessary. The golden question is, which one do you feed the *wants* and *desires*? Is it the eye, the soul or the spirit?

Every day, you have that conflict going on between all three. Part of your journey on this planet is to achieve a balance among the three entities. Your eyes represent the physical aspect of things

Ascend to Your Higher Self.

in the material world. Your soul is your thinking, your mentality, your mindset. Your spirit represents the real you.

You see.

You want.

You desire.

You get.

What are you going to do? Who will you feed? Would it be your eyes, your soul/mind, or your spirit?

Ascend to Your Higher Self.

Chapter 15

The characteristic energetic frequency with which money exhibits is inversely proportional to any form of doubt.

—Samuel K. Anderson

Ascend to Your Higher Self.

The characteristic energetic frequency of money increases as your doubt towards it decreases. The frequency reduces drastically as your doubts increases rapidly.

You will need to comprehend who you are as an energy force. You attract and repel other forms of energy as you move around daily.

Everything about you constitutes energy. Your thoughts, your actions, your

Ascend to Your Higher Self.

words and your entire existence. The more you become aware of your being; the more you become aware of the power hidden within you to command, demand and speak things into existence. It's a journey.

When you become too anxious about money then money will repel from you. Regardless of how you received or attained the money; when the energy is not right, you will lose it all.

Ascend to Your Higher Self.

Chapter 16

At the end of it all before exiting this earth, regardless of how you exit; make sure that you smile and if possible laugh believing and knowing that you came into this life, you saw exactly what it's all about, you lived it up and you conquered.

-Samuel K. Anderson

Ascend to Your Higher Self.

Every journey eventually comes to an end sooner or later. This experience called life on earth will also end. In this flesh, we will all wave goodbye to our love ones, friends or colleagues.

You are born, you crawl, you talk, you walk, you live (some choose to just exist) and eventually; we all exit from the flesh (body).

What legacy are you going to leave behind for posterity? What kind of lifestyle are you pushing right now?

Ascend to Your Higher Self.

Think about life as a responsibility that requires accountability. Live it with a cause, a purpose and one that is worth living.

In the end, make sure you exit the stage with a smile married with no regrets. You are reading this right now, that means you still have the opportunity to live your life with no regret(s).

Ascend to Your Higher Self.

Chapter 17

You must go through the moments, emotions, and spirituality in order to get your blessings.

Let your mind, emotions, body and spirit be your guide.

~Samuel K. Anderson

Ascend to Your Higher Self.

Blessings are all around us just like the air we breathe. So, why do some people feel blessed while others feel the opposite?

Have the right mindset when going through the "MES" (moments, emotions, spirituality) to get the blessings. We all go through the emotions of joy, boredom, excitement, envy, surprises, romance, horror, sadness, anger, loss, disgust, fear, contempt, confusion, triumph, etc. These experiences are made up of moments that sometimes bring us to our knees. However, you have to mentally train yourself to stand tall and remain calm.

There should be a balance between your spiritual aura, physical (body) aura, emotional aura, and mental or psychological aura. The balance comes with daily practice to think positively in every situation especially during moments of weary and heaviness. Remember to be good to yourself.

Ascend to Your Higher Self.

Chapter 18

Extinction of humans precedes nature's extinction.

—Samuel K. Anderson

Ascend to Your Higher Self.

Destruction of nature is directly proportional to destruction of human beings. Every bit of nature destroyed is a direct destruction to humans. To cause deforestation without afforestation is to cause intentional food starvation to humans without the intent to nutritiously replenish them in any shape or form.

The solution to every problem is found within the cause of the problem. So, show me all the causes to a problem, list them down, and I will easily show you the solution(s) to the problems. The fact still remains that nature was here before humans and nature will still be here after humans are gone regardless of the magnitude of effects our uncivilized acts may cause to nature.

That is to say, extinction of humans precedes nature's extinction. Our oneness with nature and the universe is inevitable.

Ascend to Your Higher Self.

Chapter 19

Every object living or non-living contains energy that vibrates in its unique frequency mimicking its directional flow of its core energy.

—Samuel K. Anderson

Ascend to Your Higher Self.

The frequency at which any object vibrates is linked to the behavioral exhibition of the object's energy. Energy is the life-source of everything that exist in the universe.

Your core energy is vital to your balance in the universe. Reset, refresh, recharge or renew your vibrations to make sure that you are in alignment with your core energy.

Ascend to Your Higher Self.

Chapter 20

Every living thing with flesh or physical body on earth has components of sand (soil).

—Samuel K. Anderson

Ascend to Your Higher Self.

Fruits, vegetables, plants, fishes, animals, humans, and all other living organisms with a body or flesh decompose into soil after the *energy* in them is transferred to a different state in the universe.

We burry the seed of a plant in the soil for it to rot in order to germinate. After germination, the young plant needs air, water and sunlight to grow. Chlorophyll in green plants uses energy from the sun to trigger photosynthesis.

Ascend to Your Higher Self.

Every living organism depends on each other for energy. The energy is what keeps every living thing alive. There are different kinds of energy needed for survival. The body or flesh of all the living things are useless without the presence of energies in them.

At the end of it all, every living thing returns back into the soil(ground) as the energy is released into the universe for its next cycle within another body.

Ascend to Your Higher Self.

Chapter 21

My pedagogy is my pedagogy and my pedagogy only.

—Samuel K. Anderson

What is your pedagogy? You ought to have and know your pedagogy. Pedagogy applies to your methodological practice of teaching not limited to academics but also to your social, moral, psychological, spiritual and theoretical concept of existence.

Some attribute five approaches to classify pedagogy, namely: reflective approach, inquiry approach, constructivism or constructivist approach, collaborative approach and integrative approach. In simplicity, pedagogy can be directly linked to leadership. The mother and father play the role as leaders in leading their child/children. Big and small groups or organizations have those that lead them with agreed upon missions and visions. In the classroom, the teacher becomes the leader in directing or teaching the school children.

Ascend to Your Higher Self.

Chapter 22

When it's TIME for TIME to reveal its TIME for what it has TIMED then it's TIME. When it's TIME it's TIME.

~Samuel K. Anderson

Ascend to Your Higher Self.

When it's time it's time.

When it's time, time will trigger its time to be in line with your coordinated time without affecting the perfect universal equilibrium frequency of time that vibrates through all energies rendering solace in oneness of peace and harmony.

Time is best put as existence in nonexistence and nonexistence in existence. There is no gap or space within time. Our perceptions of time create the kind of time we experience. Time is neither fast nor slow, calm or wild, long or short, exist or nonexistent, thin or wide and time is definitely not old or new. Time in your perceived reality is a reality of unreality. The perception of the "age" of time on a body is the freedom of the soul and spirit to be set free completely.

When it's time it's time. It has always been your time even prior to your perceived conception of time. Your

Ascend to Your Higher Self.

perception created an unrealistic delay in your sub-universe that has been waiting to connect to the grand universe. There is no time within time but a perceived time within time. At the heart of time nothing exists yet everything exists in time concurrently.

Your journey doesn't end when you physically die rather it only begins. To die is to live and to live is to die. When it's time it's time. Your time is when your mind is fully connected to time and that's when you begin to live.

Ascend to Your Higher Self.

Chapter 23

Resonate with the renaissance of intellectual, cultural, spiritual and social vibrations of the frequency energetically permeating through the old worlds and the new era to re-set the universe to its futuristic wholeness of yesteryears just as it was in the beginning.

– Samuel K. Anderson

Ascend to Your Higher Self.

Reverberating of electrical resonance from your medulla oblongata and the pineal gland is pivotal to initiating your renaissance in your intellectual, cultural, spiritual, and social wellbeing.

Breath in, breath out. Go deep into your soul and spirit to be in unison with your body and get ready to travel through the predestined frequencies vibrating within you. Yes, you should be able to feel it

Ascend to Your Higher Self.

around you too. That's the energetic frequency needed to vibrate your aura. Your old self, your present self and your future self can be experienced all at once within this renaissance of intellectual, cultural, spiritual and social vibrations. Everything is made clear in this realm. You are as you were made to be from the beginning of your existence. Consistently meditate with no distractions to wheel yourself into it.

Ascend to Your Higher Self.

Chapter 24

The most powerful weapon effective to destabilizing the strength, power, intellectual agility, and the union of any friendship, relationship, family, community, institutions, municipality, a state/region or a nation is the seed of discord.

—Samuel K. Anderson

Ascend to Your Higher Self.

The most powerful weapon effective to destabilizing the strength, power, intellectual agility, and the union of any friendship, relationship, family, community, institutions, municipality, a state/region or a nation is the seed of discord. Once effectively sowed, you can easily control, manipulate and destroy such people's identity, confidence, knowledge and their very worth. Such distorted people will believe anything outside of themselves.

This is an excerpt from the book *Whispers from My Mother* by Samuel K. Anderson. *(My Book – kindly check it out)*

Chapter 25

Who you are is not who you THINK you are, who you are is who you KNOW you are.

~Samuel K. Anderson

Ascend to Your Higher Self.

Let me break it down!!!

Know: This is your awareness of spiritual, psychological, emotional, physical, cultural and traditional development. Your core that is deeply embedded in your root. Knowing who you are also means that you spend time with yourself to establish an *agape* type of love, respect and honor about your mission, vision and execution. In this state of self-awareness, you are one hundred and ten percent convinced, connected and sure of your entire being.

Think: You are consumed with uncertainties about who you are culturally, spiritually, psychologically, emotionally, physically, and traditionally. You tend to be at cross roads. Sadly, you seem to be a prisoner of others' opinions of you, lies from all the misinformation and miseducation, uncertainty of your purpose, etc.

Ascend to Your Higher Self.

Chapter 26

I am a *MASTER* of the things I know and a *STUDENT* of the things I do not know.

~Samuel K. Anderson

Ascend to Your Higher Self.

You may very well know about the old adage that goes like this "*a jack of all trades and a master of none*".

In my experiences through life I have rather come to *know* that *I am a jack of all trades and a <u>master of many</u>*.

I achieved this level of intellectual frequency by continuously daring to intensely research, study, learn and question everything by applying the questioning of "*when*", "*how*", "*who*", "*what*".

Ascend to Your Higher Self.

The word "etymology" should be your best buddy when it comes to your intellectual-archaeological digging of information. Be humbly enthused and hungrily determined about the opportunities to learn, study and research as a student of the things you do not know in order to become a master of the things you will eventually know. Lastly, my life experiences are nothing shy of tough, hard, brutal, painful and critical. I have learned a lot from life.

Ascend to Your Higher Self.

Chapter 27

Invest in the SANITY, SANCTITY and SANCTUARY of your mind

— Samuel K. Anderson

Ascend to Your Higher Self.

Psychological health is key for you to succeed in this life. I highly encourage you to take time to rest, focus, motivate yourself, and believe in yourself. You ought to believe that you are capable and worth it. Cut of all the distractions. Do not waste your energy on the naysayers. Doubt steals the essence in your relevance. Hence, make sure to believe in yourself, show some faith and desire to exhibit your capabilities. You are here, alive, and healthy. Invest in the sanity, sanctity and sanctuary of your mind.

Ascend to Your Higher Self.

Chapter 28

These three things are principal for you to succeed: Identifying your gift, Kickstarting your action of execution, and consistency.

~Samuel K. Anderson

Ascend to Your Higher Self.

Identifying your gift: You were born with a gift. You cannot buy it. It is rather unique to you because it was specifically imbedded in you right from your conception. Dig within you to identify this gift.

Kickstarting your action of execution: Believe in your gift enough to take bold steps to bring it into fruition. You will need to be confident to exercise your gift. Practice it consistently.

Consistency: You are prone to mess up probably over and over again from the beginning. However, that should not stop you. Make sure you keep on keeping on. Consistency is key in this journey.

Ascend to Your Higher Self.

Chapter 29

God is a man.

Adam/Adama = Male & Female.

God created "Adam/Adama" in His (God's) image and likeness. You are not equal to God but a direct part of God. Hence, you are eternal and a god.

~Samuel K. Anderson

To explain this piece in this chapter, I would like to simply infuse a section that I wrote from my book "Whispers from My Mother"

"I am a god!
Yes, I am a god.
How? Why? Because, I am a "god" product of "The God"
We are all gods with specific responsibilities under the sun.
Some are lost gods with lost identities trying and searching to identify their purpose and being.

Ascend to Your Higher Self.

The "god" can never be greater than "The God"
For it is out of the existence of "The God" that the "god" exists.
A lost god will struggle to identify with "The God" unless the lost god finds his/her "purpose" of existence in direct relation to "The God".

"The God" is everything.
I am then an energy
I am a force
I am a spirit
I am a god."

Samuel K. Anderson (Whispers from My Mother)

Ascend to Your Higher Self.

Chapter 30

He who panics dramatically decreases his chances to overcome the challenge at hand.

~Samuel K. Anderson

Ascend to Your Higher Self.

Seek knowledge, research, embrace wisdom and no matter the weight of the challenge at hand; make sure to not be afraid. In that, knowledge, research and wisdom are some of the top remedies to counter most of our dilemmas.

To ascend to your higher self is to be able to allow your *energy* to *vibrate* high enough to propel you into a higher *frequency* of your true self. I call this the ability to experience your *energetic vibrating frequency*.

I encourage you to always remember this truth: The easiest way to get a weak immune system making you more susceptible to ailments is continuous panic. Panic begets fear and in turn fear begets stress.

Stress releases the cortisol hormones. High cortisol makes you extremely susceptible to infections and diseases. Do not panic. Do not fear. Do not stress.

Ascend to Your Higher Self.

The
END

Ascend to Your Higher Self.

Samuel K. Anderson (MBA, BSBA, University of The Incarnate Word) is a Ghanaian Nigerian American citizen and a member of the largest leadership honor society in the nation (United States of America) known as NSLS, The National Society of Leadership and Success. He has served as an astute leader, motivator, philanthropist, father, entrepreneur, mentor, wisdom seeker and educator.

He is a vibrant CEO and founder of two companies. A motivational and life coach speaker. He has impeccable hands on experience in banking, real estate, bankruptcy, life insurance, compliance, risk management, estate, probate, foreclosure, and investments. He served in his early formal education years as the Regional Trustee for the Eastern Regional Students' Representative Council with the Council's aim to Emancipate Students through Dialogue and a Philosophy of Non-Violence, President of an NGO that aimed at educating the youths on drug abuse, Counselor and Director of Children's Ministry. He completed formal bible training education/Seminary School and also studied Theology at Central University College before transitioning to San Antonio College then transferred to University of The Incarnate Word to pursue bachelor's degree in Accounting and an MBA with concentration in Asset Management (Real Estate and Finance).

Kindly contact me: samuelkanderson777@outlook.com **with your specific requirements for speaking events.**

www.ingramcontent.com/pod-product-compliance
Lightning Source LLC
Chambersburg PA
CBHW071022080526
44587CB00015B/2458